MICHAEL JORDAN

BASKETBALL LEGEND

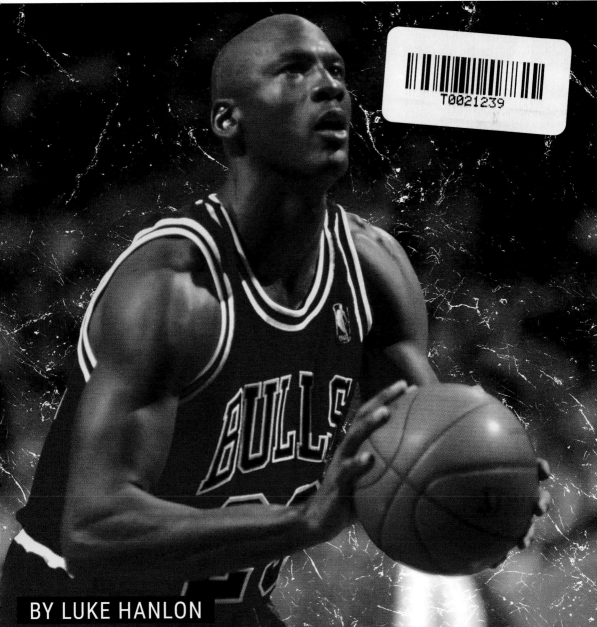

BY LUKE HANLON

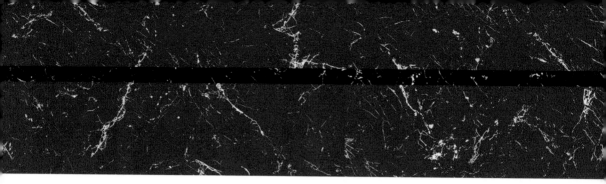

Book design by Jake Nordby
Cover design by Jake Nordby

Photographs ©: Tom DiPace/AP Images, cover, 1; Mark J. Terrill/AP Images, 4; Mark Welsh/Arlington Heights Daily Herald/AP Images, 7; Robert Willett/Raleigh News and Observer/AP Images, 8–9; Bettmann/Getty Images, 11, 12, 17; John Swart/AP Images, 14, 30; Reed Saxon/AP Images, 18; Kathy Willens/AP Images, 20–21; Mark Elias/AP Images, 22; Charles Bennett/AP Images, 25; Brian Bahr/Allsport/Getty Images Sport/Getty Images, 27; Red Line Editorial, 29

Press Box Books, an imprint of Press Room Editions.

ISBN
978-1-63494-789-3 (library bound)
978-1-63494-809-8 (paperback)
978-1-63494-848-7 (epub)
978-1-63494-829-6 (hosted ebook)

Library of Congress Control Number: 2023908987

Distributed by North Star Editions, Inc.
2297 Waters Drive
Mendota Heights, MN 55120
www.northstareditions.com

Printed in the United States of America
012024

About the Author

Luke Hanlon is a sportswriter and editor based in Minneapolis.

TABLE OF CONTENTS

1 SIX-FOR-SIX

Michael Jordan watched intently as Utah Jazz power forward Karl Malone grabbed the ball in the post. Then, Jordan's defensive instincts kicked in. The Chicago Bulls guard broke free from the player he was guarding. He caught Malone by surprise from behind. After one quick swipe from Jordan, the Bulls had the ball back.

Only 20 seconds remained in Game 6 of the 1998 National Basketball Association (NBA) Finals. The Jazz were

In the 1998 NBA Finals, Michael Jordan led all players with 33.5 points per game.

leading 86–85. But the Chicago Bulls led the series 3–2. A win in Utah would clinch Jordan's sixth NBA title.

The seconds ticked away. Jordan dribbled the ball while waiting behind the three-point line. He had already scored 43 points in the game. But Jordan wasn't done. Utah forward Bryon Russell moved in to slow Jordan. With one hard dribble to the right, Jordan burst past the Utah defender. Then Jordan stopped and quickly dribbled the ball back to his left hand. The move left Russell on the floor.

From the top of the key, Jordan calmly rose into the air for a jump shot. He held his shooting arm in the air until the ball hit nothing but net. The stunned Utah fans went silent.

The Jazz had one last chance to force a Game 7. Point guard John Stockton's

Jordan celebrates after winning Game 6 of the 1998 NBA Finals.

last-second heave clanked off the rim. The

Bulls were NBA champions for the third straight

year. And for the sixth time, Jordan was named

Finals Most Valuable Player (MVP).

2 CAROLINA KID

Michael Jordan was born on February 17, 1963, in Brooklyn, New York. However, his family moved to North Carolina a few years later. There, Michael attended Laney High School in Wilmington. That was where he first played basketball.

Michael wasn't a superstar right away. As a sophomore, he stood 5-foot-10 (178 cm) and couldn't dunk. The varsity coach didn't think he was ready. Being cut from the team stung Michael. But he used

A young Michael Jordan (23) stands with North Carolina coach Dean Smith and teammates.

it as motivation to work hard and get better. Michael made the varsity team the next year. By the end of his high school career, many top college teams wanted him. Michael decided to stay in his home state and play for the University of North Carolina.

Coach Dean Smith had built a strong program. Behind budding star James Worthy, the Tar Heels had reached the 1981 national championship game. When Jordan arrived in 1981–82, he fit in right away. The freshman averaged 13.5 points per game while helping the Tar Heels reach the national championship game again. They faced a strong Georgetown University team. The Hoyas featured a superstar freshman of their own, center Patrick Ewing.

With 53 seconds left, the Hoyas led 62–61. North Carolina needed a basket to

Jordan takes the game-winning shot in the 1982 national championship game.

stay alive. The Tar Heels looked to their star

freshman. And Jordan delivered. His difficult

shot from the left wing put North Carolina up

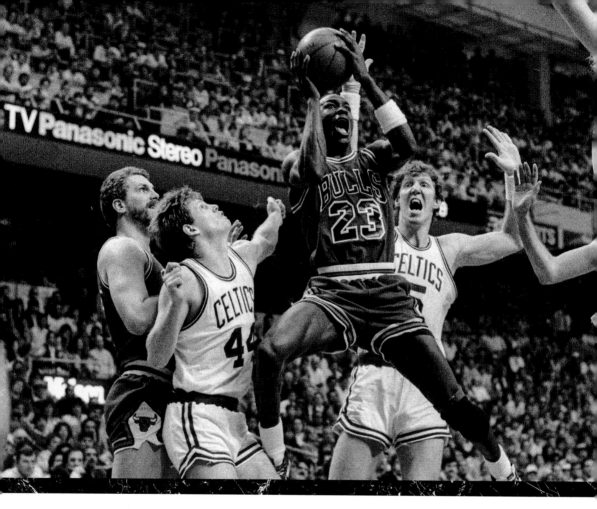

Jordan takes a shot against the Boston Celtics in the 1986 playoffs.

63–62 with 16 seconds left. It proved to be the championship-winning shot.

Jordan spent two more years with the Tar Heels. As a junior, he was named the national player of the year. That summer, the Chicago

Bulls selected Jordan with the third overall pick in the 1984 NBA Draft.

With his athletic frame and superb quickness, Jordan took the league by storm. In the 1984–85 season, Jordan averaged 28.2 points per game and was the NBA Rookie of the Year. By his third season in 1986–87, he averaged a league-high 37.1 points per game. That was one of the highest scoring averages in a season in NBA history. However, Chicago was still finding its footing. The Boston Celtics swept the Bulls in the first round of the playoffs for the second straight year.

BUDDING STAR

The Bulls faced the powerhouse Boston Celtics in the opening round of the 1986 playoffs. Michael Jordan scored 49 points in Game 1. He was even better in Game 2. Jordan scored 63 points, the most scored in a playoff game ever. Celtics forward Larry Bird was amazed by Jordan's performance. "It's just God disguised as Michael Jordan," Bird said after the game.

3 AIR JORDAN

By 1987–88, Michael Jordan had established himself as one of the NBA's most dangerous players. He won the second of seven consecutive scoring titles that season. As a lockdown defender, he led the league with 3.2 steals per game. Plus, no player averaged more minutes per game. It all added up to help Jordan earn his first NBA MVP Award. But he still needed to prove that he could lead a playoff push.

Jordan performs at the dunk contest during the 1988 NBA All-Star Weekend.

After beating them in the first round the previous year, the Bulls faced the Cleveland Cavaliers to open the 1989 postseason. Trailing 100–99 late in a winner-take-all Game 5, Jordan took control. With three seconds left, he received an inbound pass and quickly pulled up for a shot. The ball left Jordan's hands just before the final buzzer sounded. It rattled around the rim before sinking through the net. Jordan leaped into the air, pumping his fist in celebration as the Bulls advanced. This moment became known as "The Shot."

Eventually, the Bulls went up against the bruising Detroit Pistons in the conference finals. Detroit had knocked them out of the playoffs in five games the year before. Detroit used a physical defensive style to slow Jordan's scoring. And it worked. The Pistons won in

Jordan dunks over a Cleveland player in the 1989 playoffs.

six games. The Pistons then eliminated Chicago in the 1990 conference finals as well.

During that 1990 off-season, Jordan added muscle. He practiced his scoring in the post. All the work paid off. The Bulls once again met the

Jordan is surrounded by media members after winning the 1991 NBA Finals.

Pistons in the 1991 conference finals. This time Jordan averaged 29.8 points as the Bulls swept the series.

The Bulls met the Los Angeles Lakers in the 1991 NBA Finals. Lakers point guard Magic Johnson had been the league's biggest star in the 1980s. Now, Jordan had a chance to take the throne. He did just that, averaging more than 31 points and 11 assists per game as the Bulls won in five games.

Jordan was only getting started. He led the Bulls to victory in the 1992 and 1993 NBA Finals as well. Each time, Jordan was named Finals MVP. In 1990–91 and 1991–92, he was named NBA MVP as well. The Bulls became the first team to win three straight NBA championships since 1966. Perhaps no athlete in the world was as famous as Michael Jordan.

DREAM TEAM

Michael Jordan was on top of the NBA in 1992. That summer, he turned into a global superstar as well. Jordan starred alongside 10 other future Hall of Famers on the US "Dream Team" at the 1992 Olympics in Barcelona, Spain. Mobs of fans followed the players around as the United States marched on to the gold medal. Many credit the Dream Team with popularizing basketball around the world.

JORDAN BRAND

Michael Jordan had unmatched skills on the court. It turned out he had one-of-a-kind marketability off the court, too. In 1985, Nike released shoes specifically for Jordan called the Air Jordan 1. Millions of pairs were sold in the shoe's first year.

By 1986–87, Nike began to release signature Jordan shoes each season. They became popular enough for Jordan to branch off with his own brand in 1997. The popularity of Jordan's shoes has also inspired modern NBA athletes. Many stars have their own signature shoes.

Jordan was a big name for more than just shoes, though. In 1991, Gatorade signed a deal with Jordan to make him the sports drink's first sponsored athlete. After he starred in a commercial with the tagline "Be Like Mike," the drink's popularity skyrocketed around the world. Throughout his career, Jordan also had sponsorship deals with Coca-Cola, Wheaties, McDonald's, and other major brands.

On September 9, 1997, Jordan holds his signature shoe at a press conference announcing his brand.

4 THE G.O.A.T.

Tragedy struck Michael Jordan in July 1993. His father, James, was killed in North Carolina. In the prime of his career, Jordan questioned if he still wanted to play basketball. On October 6, 1993, he shocked the sports world when he retired from the NBA at age 30.

Jordan said that he needed a new challenge in his life. He had enjoyed playing baseball as a kid. The Chicago White Sox offered him an opportunity to try the sport professionally. Jordan

An emotional Jordan addresses the media at his retirement press conference in 1993.

played in the minor leagues in 1994. However, he struggled on the baseball diamond. On March 19, 1995, Jordan returned to the NBA.

It took some time for Jordan to be back at full strength. By 1995–96, it was like he'd never left. At age 32, Jordan won his eighth NBA scoring title and fourth MVP Award. Along with longtime sidekick Scottie Pippen, Jordan led the Bulls to an NBA-record 72 regular-season wins. After losing once in the opening three rounds of the playoffs, the Bulls faced the Seattle SuperSonics in the Finals. Like clockwork, Jordan won another Finals MVP Award.

SPACE JAM

Already an NBA superstar, Michael Jordan turned into a movie star in 1996. That November, Space Jam hit theaters around the world. Jordan starred as himself and played basketball with Bugs Bunny and other Looney Tunes characters. It was incredibly popular and earned more than $230 million worldwide.

Jordan clutches the ball moments after winning Game 6 of the 1996 NBA Finals.

The Bulls clinched the championship on Father's Day. Afterward, an emotional Jordan wept on the floor with the game ball in his hands.

The Bulls made it back to the Finals in 1997. They faced the Utah Jazz. With the series tied, Jordan began feeling ill ahead of Game 5 in Utah. He battled through the flu-like symptoms and scored a game-high 38 points. That included a three-pointer to give the Bulls the lead with 25 seconds left. After winning the "Flu Game," the Bulls won Game 6 to secure Jordan's fifth championship. Then Jordan and the Bulls defeated the Jazz again in 1998 to clinch another three-peat. In all six wins, Jordan was named Finals MVP.

Jordan dominated the NBA like no player had before him. After the 1998 Finals, he retired again. And once again, he came back. He played two seasons with the Washington Wizards, earning All-Star selections both times. Finally, he retired for the last time in 2003.

Jordan averaged 32.3 points per game in the 1997 NBA Finals.

Jordan remained a global icon. People still lined up to buy Jordan Brand shoes and other products he endorsed. In 2010, he bought the Charlotte Bobcats (now Hornets). The purchase made Jordan the first NBA majority owner who used to play in the league. Even after his career, Jordan was still making history.

TIMELINE

1. Brooklyn, New York (February 17, 1963)
Michael Jordan is born. A few years later, he moves to Wilmington, North Carolina.

2. New Orleans, Louisiana (March 29, 1982)
Jordan wins the national championship with the University of North Carolina.

3. Chicago, Illinois (October 26, 1984)
After being selected with the third overall pick in the NBA Draft, Jordan makes his debut for the Chicago Bulls.

4. Cleveland, Ohio (May 7, 1989)
Jordan hits "The Shot" to win a playoff series against the Cleveland Cavaliers.

5. Inglewood, California (June 12, 1991)
Jordan leads the Bulls to their first championship, defeating the Los Angeles Lakers in five games.

6. Salt Lake City, Utah (June 14, 1998)
Jordan makes his final shot with the Bulls and beats the Utah Jazz, winning his sixth championship.

7. Washington, DC (April 16, 2003)
Jordan retires for the last time after two seasons with the Washington Wizards.

8. Charlotte, North Carolina (February 27, 2010)
Jordan officially becomes the majority owner of the Charlotte Bobcats (now Hornets).

Birth date: February 17, 1963

Birthplace: Brooklyn, New York

Position: Shooting guard

Size: 6-foot-6 (198 cm), 198 pounds (90 kg)

Teams: North Carolina Tar Heels (1981–84), Chicago Bulls (1984–93, 1995–98), Washington Wizards (2001–03)

Major awards: NBA MVP (1988, 1991–92, 1996, 1998), NBA Finals MVP (1991–93, 1996–98), NBA scoring title (1987–93, 1996–98), NBA Rookie of the Year (1985), NBA Defensive Player of the Year (1988), Basketball Hall of Fame (2009)

GLOSSARY

assists
Passes that lead directly to a teammate scoring a basket.

conference
A smaller group of teams that make up part of a sports league.

majority owner
The person that controls more than half of an organization.

marketability
Having a quality that is appealing to customers.

post
The area close to the basket where taller players usually play.

rookie
A first-year player.

swept
Won every game in a series.

varsity
The top team in a sport at a high school.

TO LEARN MORE

Books

Flynn, Brendan. *Chicago Bulls All-Time Greats*. Mankato, MN: Press Box Books, 2020.

Greenberg, Keith Elliot. *LeBron James vs. Michael Jordan: Who Would Win?* Minneapolis: Lerner Publications, 2024.

Kjartansson, Kjartan Atli. *Legends of the NBA*. New York: Abbeville Kids, 2022.

More Information

To learn more about Michael Jordan, go to **pressboxbooks.com/AllAccess**.

These links are routinely monitored and updated to provide the most current information available.

INDEX